C000045690

There's Sub-Thing About Subbing...

PALMETTO

PUBLISHING

Charleston, SC

www.PalmettoPublishing.com

Copyright © 2024 by P.M. Riv

All rights reserved.

No portion of this book may be reproduced, stored in a retrieval system, or transmitted in any form by any means–electronic, mechanical, photocopy, recording, or other–except for brief quotations in printed reviews, without prior permission of the author.

Hardcover ISBN: 979-8-8229-4327-8

Paperback ISBN: 979-8-8229-4328-5

There's Sub-Thing About Subbing....

Hilarious little stories from a real-live Substitute Teacher...The World's Greatest Substitute Teacher of all Time...ha, not really, but maybe...

by P.M. Riv

SHOUT OUT–

I would like to dedicate this book to all of the amazing teachers, substitute teachers, and staff members.
I am truly blessed to work with the best of the best...Love you guys...and you know who you are...

Preface

A little pre diddy (also known as a preface...HA!)

I can't believe, I am finally writing "the book," that I have said I was going to write for a gazillion years. Well, it is summertime, mid July 2023, and what better time to start when you are OFF for the summer...'cause yah know, I'm a substitute teacher...

I have been subbing just under ten years...somewhere around there...in the northwest side of a "really big city." I started subbing in a Catholic school and ventured my way to a public school after a few years. I enjoy the flexibility and changing of the guard between the different schools.

A few quick housekeeping notes before you get started:

I am very very sarcastic, always "kidding" just jokin'...ok? It's all good; don't be scared; you can do it...just read these stories and laugh; that's it...ok????

I am going to shorten substitute to sub—BECAUSE it's easier—just wanted to clarify that for you...

I will not be using real names, to protect all humans involved in the craziness. Mmmmmm, perhaps I will use the fake names like, Zuzu and FreddyFuFu, when referring to student stories. Let's see where the stories take us; I will mix it up and use different names as we progress through the book. Hope you are all ok with the names; I don't want to OFFEND anyone. Everyone is so sensitive today...yeeeeshk...

Student stories will be categorized by "Itty Bittys," "The Mids," and "The Big Kids." You will get it...just keep reading...

I might have swear words in the book, sorry, not sorry...I think you will be ok...if you aren't, then put the fkn book down! (HA.)

Definition of a "shitty" parent: One who doesn't give a shit about their kid. Not sure _why_ you have kids to be honest, 'cause you really suck at it. Throughout this book, you will see "shitty parent alert." There will be many examples of a shitty parent. For those who are good parents, this will not offend you or piss you off. For those who are actually shitty parents, well, um, yeah, this will probably offend the FK out of you...Relax, it's all good, and maybe you will learn a thing or two from this crazy sub teacher. LOL...

Part I

The Itty-Bittys

**(aka: pre-K4, kindergartners, first graders, second graders.
I am known as Mrs. Patti, Mrs. M., teacher-teacher)**

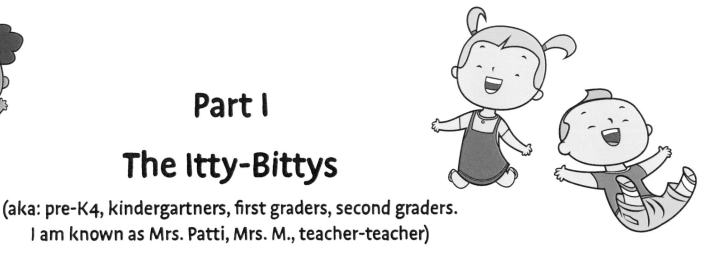

36-Yep-36

It's my first day subbing at the *public school,* I am nervous as hell, it's hotter than a cat's ass, and I'm sweating bullets already...

I approach the school clerk in the office, say good morning, and introduce myself. The clerk, who is very sweet and helpful, lets me know the kindergarten classroom number and points down the hallway.

I enter the room, look around, and say to myself, SHIT there are a ton of tables and chairs; this can't be the number of students, right? (I am used to teaching smaller class sizes in Catholic schools.)

I quickly open the Sub-Plans, which are basically what you will be doing for the day with the precious Itty-Bittys.

I know it will be an interesting day when I read the *special notes* section. It stated, "Beware of 'FreddyFuFu.' He is a challenge; you need to say his name twice, 'FreddyFuFu, FreddyFuFu,' in order to get his attention. He sits in a special chair and desk, away from the other students, due to his outbursts and challenging behavior."

Ohhhhhh greattttttttt this is going to be fun. Ok, so I start to get nervous sweats now. You know what those are. I'm sure you have experienced them; your breathing increases, you start to sweat pebbles down your cheeks, and your stomach hurts like you have to take a dump...

I quickly go through the remainder of the sub plans, and then I come to the attendance roster. WHAT THE FK!! Thirty-six kindergartners?????? This must be a mistake, or wait. I'm sure I will have a kindergarten aide, just like in the Catholic schools. Ok phew, I'll be ok once she gets here.

I look at the clock—two minutes until the precious angels enter the building. I'm confused. Where is my aide? I quickly go to the office and ask the sweet, lovely clerk, "What time does the kindergarten aide get here?" She looks at me with a warm, nervous smile, "I'm sorry, we don't have kindergarten aides at our school; you will be by yourself."

WHHHHHHHHAAAAAAAAATTTTTTTTTTTT??????

I calmly go back to the classroom, say a prayer, and RRRRRIIIINNNNGGGG, here they come!!

One by one, they come in the classroom door, and I am smiling, saying good morning, as my vision starts to go to a slow-motion blurrrrr.

Each child is coming in slow motion, blurring their words...gggggooooodddddmmmmooooorrrrrrnnnnnniiiinnnnnnggggg.

They just keep coming, and coming, and coming—it just doesn't stop! It feels like four hours have gone by, and they are still coming in the door.

Ok, that's thirty-five so far, and here comes...AHHHHHHHHHHHHHHHHHHHH!

A huge screamer, running in the classroom—yep, it is FreddyFuFu.

The thirty-sixth student.

Sidebar-It never fails; whenever I am subbing, THEY ALL SHOW UP!

First things first, FreddyFuFu (I state his name twice, damn it, and he's not listening…1-800-givethiskidsomebenadryl!!!!)

FreddyFuFu finally calms down and is sitting at his special chair and desk.

Yep, I have thirty-six kindergartners today, by myself, and it's not even 9:00 a.m.

"Ok, class, I'm turning off the lights again—brain break!"

Sub plans say I can give one or two brain breaks throughout the day to help settle the class down.

Well, after the forty-fifth brain break, I think the hyperactivity level has gone down maybe two decibels. (Lord help me.)

Art time: ZuZu cuts her hair, FreddyFuFu swallows glue, BoBo literally slams his entire body on the table and explodes all the art projects, LollyLa eats her Play-Doh, and Jiffy sticks his pencil up his nose and cries bloody murder because he can't get it out!

One adorable student comes up to me and says, "Mrs. Patti, I think I know why our teacher isn't here today. She probably has a bad headache…we are really crazy in here…" This is truly the highlight of my day…

Trying to teach this class has been probably one of the craziest days of my subbing career, a day I will never forget.

I go home and tell my husband I am going to bed. I fall on the bed, like Arnold Schwarzenegger does in the movie, *Kindergarten Cop,* and pass out. It is maybe 5:23 p.m.

Sidebar-As a sub, you have to remember, when you are teaching the Itty-Bittys, you are always "ON;" they constantly want to be entertained and want your attention. It's exhausting but rewarding at the same time. I enjoy the Ittys; most of them listen to you—most, not all, but most.

BooBoo On Vacation

First grader, we will call him BooBoo; no he wasn't like that, "Oh, what a cute little BooBoo." He was awful...It's Tuesday morning, and the teacher wants to be sure that I go through his weekend take-home folder. He is behind in a lot of work and was supposed to have done it over the weekend. It was a "long holiday weekend." I start going through his folder, and it is FULL of homework, that has not been touched.

Shitty Parent Alert
Parents, can you PLEASE go through your child's take-home folder, especially the Itty-Bittys'. I have seen notes that were supposed to be signed from September, and it is now MAY...Come onnnnnnnnnaaaaaaaa...

Back to BooBoo's folder. I look at BooBoo and ask him why he didn't do his homework. BooBoo looks at me, (he's this chubby kid with an attitude) raises both hands in the air, and says, "Mrs. Patti, I was on vacation!" It takes everything in me not to crack up right then and there, but I hold my composure, barely. I say, "Oh really? How nice. Where was vacation?" They had gone to Wisconsin Dells for the long weekend, and he even shows me his wristband for the crazy wavy pool. He then tells me he hasn't showered and wants to keep the wristband on forever. "OK!"

Time for a kindergartner joke:

What kind of bear do you find in the kitchen?

A Pan-Da

SideBar-I sub this crazy, crazy, crazy Itty-Bitty class, several times. The stories just never stop; there is always something EVERY TIME I SUB THIS CLASS. There are so many times I want to jump into my *Sam Kinison* role and say to the class, "SHUTUUUUUUUUP!"

Don't worry, I never did… (HA.)

BigBoy

There is a very big boy—really really big for his age—so we will call him BigBoy. BigBoy cannot sit still in his seat and is always kneeling on his chair, diving over his desk, and crashing the other students' pencil cases and materials to the ground. One day, BigBoy comes up to me, and he isn't feeling well. He really doesn't look very well—cheeks flush and rosy, coughing, snotty nose, the whole nine yards. I send him to the nurse. He comes back five minutes later. The nurse says no fever, seems fine, see how he is after lunch. "OK!" It's now after lunch. BigBoy comes up to me; "Mrs. Patti, I just puked in the hallway." "OK!" I have BigBoy go back to the nurse. The nurse comes in my classroom, "BigBoy is going home." "OK!"

I finally see the cleaning person (we used to call them janitors when I was growing up, but now they have official titles) cleaning up BigBoy's puke in the hallway. What a sight…and I think I overhear on their radio, "1-ADAM-12…(remember that show? HA!)…ah yeah…BigBoy puke has been cleaned up…1-ADAM-12…Roger that…out…"

Shitty Parent Alert
When your child is sick, PLEASE, keep them at home. I know it's tough, and you have to scramble to keep a child at home. When a student comes into class and is coughing up a lung, sneezing all over his fellow students, has a fever, falls asleep on the reading rug, etc. THEY. NEED. TO. STAY. HOME.
A little note to the shitty parent: your kids tell the sub the truth.

I have heard:

"My mom gave me a ton of Tylenol flu medicine; I should be good for hours."

"My dad said not to call and bother him. Go to school sick. You will be fine."

"I think my grandma is coming at lunchtime to give me more medicine, because she told me my fever will come back after four hours."

NNNNNNNiiiiiicccccccccceeeeeeeeeeee...

Time for another kindergartner joke:

What do you call a bear without any teeth?

A gummy bear.

Back to Itty-Bittys...

SideBar-They like to get out of their seat and come up to me while I am teaching. Whenever I am with the Itty-Bittys, I set the ground rules.

"Ok class, let's pretend you have Super Glue on your chair, and you're stuck to it until lunch and recess." (HA!)

FingerCoil

There was a student, we will call him, FingerCoil. FingerCoil comes up to my desk and is in panic mode. I ask FingerCoil what is wrong...He proceeds to show me his pinky finger, with the coil from his notebook ground under his skin. FingerCoil has literally taken part of the ring-coil from his notebook and twirled it underneath his skin. I seriously do not know how he has done this without being in severe pain. Well, there goes another Itty to the nurse's office.

Oh, and yes, FingerCoil survived the outpatient school surgery and came back to class coil free...

Fer–Cry–Yi!

EraserNose

Teaching math—it's actually quiet; they are paying attention, WOW! Well, short-lived silence. EraserNose suddenly screams bloody murder. I quickly go to EraserNose and ask what is wrong. EraserNose proceeds to tell me there is something stuck way up his nose. I ask him to try to blow his nose to get it out. Not working. EraserNose proceeds to tell me he stuck his pencil way up his nose and the eraser part broke off and stayed in his nose. "OK!" I send EraserNose to the nurse. Ten minutes later, here comes EraserNose, slowwwwwly back to class. He looks like he has just run twenty laps around the school—exhausted. As he comes back to his seat, I ask if the nurse got the eraser out of his nose and if he is ok. EraserNose slowly nods his head, yes...

Broken Peanut

Teaching an absolutely, adorable pre-K four-year-old class. Really, this class is so sweet and amazing. Thank GOD for the *good classes*! Yes, there are a few. I read a book to the class titled, "Peanut the Squirrel." It is now time for recess. The kids play in a nice grassy area. They are running around, enjoying the sunshiny day, laughing, smiling—yay, recess time!

All of a sudden, DetectiveBoy comes running toward me, "Mrs. Patti, Mrs. Patti—broken Peanut, broken Peanut, broken Peanut!!!" He quickly takes me to the scene of the crime, and there lies a head with bulging eyes and body parts splattered throughout the grass. DetectiveBoy thinks it is Peanut the Squirrel. I tell him, "No, that's not broken Peanut, but Buzzy the Bunny isn't doing so well."

1-800-CUSTODIAN
911-PICKUPBUZZYBUNNYPARTS

Now that is a recess I will never forget!

Bad Words

When I first started subbing, I learned *the hard way* about asking a student, "What did they say?"

A kindergartner comes up to me and tells me ZuZu has said a bad word. I quickly ask, "What did she say?" The second he starts saying, "What the fuck," I try to stop him with my hand in the air, but it is too late.

A first grader comes up to me with a piece of paper. He tells me his buddy wrote a note with bad words. I take the note, open it up, and read the note, "SpongeBob says Fuckity Fuckity Fuckity Fuck to first grade homework." It takes everything in me not to start cracking up with laughter. I give the note to the teacher upon her return. The boys have a meeting with the teacher and parents after school. Fuckity fuck is right!!

Speaking of bad words, one of my favorite bad words is Mother FKR! I can't tell you how many times I wanted to say this in class, but don't worry; I haven't. YET!! (HA!)

Pronouncing Students' Names/Taking Attendance

I learned the hard way. But WOW, when you say a student's name wrong, you get the third degree. The student literally gets defensive, and yells back to me the *right way* to say their name.

Well, if parents didn't give their children names that sound like a genital, a queen, a king, a privileged princess, a small unknown country, etc., etc., maybe I would say their name correctly. What happened to just John, Jack, Lisa, Susan...no longer are there just the *normal* names...

Taking the easy way out in today's world, I go table to table and ask the students, "Ok, what friends are not here today at your table?" GENIUS HUH?

Time for another kindergartner joke:

What do you call a fish without eyes?

FSHHHHHHHHHH

No / Get it?? (HA!)

Part II
The Mids

(aka: third, fourth, fifth graders)

The Mids are starting to *change*. No longer Itty-Bittys, now they are in between the Itty-Bittys and the Big Kids. They are starting to listen less, have attitudes, and swear!

RichBoy

Teaching third graders today at a school with, let's say, a lot of *cayyyyshshshshshshshsh.*

It was the Monday after the Super Bowl. Yeah, I know, they still haven't made that a national holiday!! I'm tired today, so I break the ice and ask what everyone did for Super Bowl Sunday. A little Italian girl raises her hand, "I played a strip card with my family and won 100 bucks!"

"Ok, (as I am chuckling) nice job!" She gets an automatic A today in my class.

Ok—hear the *sccccrrrraaattchchch* on the record—I call on RichBoy.

RichBoy lets us all know that his parents had a really big party. They grilled out in their *indoor grill* party room. I quickly ask, "WOW, indoor grill party room?" RichBoy responds with both hands in the air, "Well, yah know Mrs. M., we do have a multi-million-dollar home."

I quickly start the lesson of the day after that response. I tell the class to get out their notebooks and write down the word, *humble,* and to give me their best definition. Perhaps RichBoy gets an F in my class today.

Time for another kindergartner joke:

Why did the pelican get kicked out of the restaurant?

Because it ran up a big "bill."

Monday Is a Holiday

Teaching fourth grade—it's a Friday, yay! The students are excited for the long weekend since they will be off on Monday, Columbus Day. AntiColumbo raises her hand and states to the class that it is also Indigenous People's Day. I confirm her statement, "Yes indeed, it was also Indigenous People's Day." AntiColumbo then expresses her feelings of not celebrating Columbus Day because he enslaved people and was horrible. I then noticed the Italian students in the back ready to go all *Tony Soprano*. (HA!) I quickly tell the class to get their science books out, and turn to page 6...whew...

Cuckoo Oil

Teaching another fourth grade science class. The discussion is about oil resources. OilGuy raises his hand and says, "We have the resources to produce our own oil, but the government is cuckoo! They don't want to open up the gates." It took everything in me not to crack up. Yep, OilGuy gets an A in science today.

Christmas Tree O Christmas Tree

It is one of those crazy days teaching both fourth and fifth grades.

Teaching fourth grade social studies, and this class just cannot sit still, be quiet, calm down. Yep, one of those classes. You know it's a crazy class when students will say, "Mrs. M., you know us, we are the crazy class of the school—everyone knows it. Mrs. M., get ready, 'cause we are nuts. It's ok, you can tell us we are awful; all the other teachers do." Whoa...next up, fifth grade. As I slowly walk into the classroom, I look up, and there is a Christmas tree hanging from the ceiling fan. The class explains to me that if you turn on the fan, the tree spins around super fast, and it hasn't fallen off the fan yet! After coming from fourth grade, this actually is a breath of fresh air and makes me laugh. Thanks for that laugh funny teacher.

Time for another kindergartner joke:

Why did the boy throw the butter out the window?

Because he wanted to see a *butter-fly*.

Part III

The Big Kids

(aka: sixth, seventh, eighth graders)

I call them the Big Kids, because the Itty-Bittys like to refer to the sixth through eighth graders as the Big Kids.

The Big Kids can be tough. They are bigger, louder, and so many of them try to outdo the others in a *class-clown* performance. There are some really amazing Big Kids too. I see future presidents, CEO's, astronauts, and save-the-world leaders in so many of them. Then there are those few—I see future breaking-news stories on the TV. (HA!)

Mrs. Pickles

Ah yes, the wonderful sixth graders coming into my classroom. This is one of those classes that you are warned about; the sub plans explain what a crazy class it is, etc...etc... I've been in here quite a few times.

In walks FacePlant; he comes in all giddy and loudly says, "Hi Mrs. Pickles!" As soon as he says that and laughs, he trips over the rug and seriously face-plants on the floor. I quickly attend to FacePlant and ask if he's ok. He gets up and is a little red in the face from embarrassment, and I would assume a little sore from the fall as well.

As the class gets settled, I quickly write the word "karma" on the board.

And so the discussion begins... (HA!)

Meow and Bark

Teaching seventh grade today. Kind of a unique little class, I must say.

We are getting into a discussion about Earth, the atmosphere, the space race, going to Mars. I am calling on students throughout the discussion. It is going pretty well until I call on KittyGirl. She answers me with a "meowwwwwww" and purrs at me. Um, ok, next student. As the discussion concludes, I call on one last student, BarkBoy. He starts to bark at me and pretends he's sniffing for a treat.

I guess this is now a thing, where kids can be animals too? I am so confused, what is this world turning into????!!!???

Next time I will have to remember dog treats and catnip for prizes. (HA!)

Haircut!

Teaching eighth grade, and it's the end of the year. Well, you know how that goes—eighth graders getting ready to graduate, and summer is on all their crazy little brains...As I am teaching one of the classes, I hear some rumbles across the hall in one of the other eighth grade classes. Our doors are open, and all of a sudden, I hear the other teacher across the hall, "Mrs. M., can you watch my class for a few minutes?" I have a second teacher in my room, so I am able to quickly go across the hallway and assist. I ask the teacher what has happened, as she is taking two students down to the office. It appears that ScissorBoy has cut SurferDude's long hair off. SurferDude shows me his now one-side-long, one-side-not-so-long hair. It is a funny, not-funny moment. Typical eighth graders...

COVID-19 Times

Ahhhh, yes, teaching *remotely* and *live/remotely*.

I pray that we won't EVER have to do this again, EVER!

Yep, even subs have to teach a class during COVID-19 due to a teacher needing to take the day off.

There are a few classic stories that I must share with all of you.

Let me provide the remote scenario for you.

I am at home on my computer, and I log onto Google Classroom. All of the students, one by one, pop up on my screen. There could be anywhere from twenty-five to thirty-five students. So it's like enlarged Brady Bunch squares all over the place. (HA!)

Memorable Moments

A second grader tells me he won't be back in the afternoon on Google Classroom because they are going to the airport and heading to Florida.

All of a sudden, the dad, who is in the background and thinks he is on mute, says, "You weren't supposed to tell the teacher that!"

First grade on Google Classroom. I am calling on certain students, and I am looking at all the *squares* to see if they are paying attention.

There's one student brushing her doll's hair; another running around playing with the dog; another one jumping on her bed; another one eating breakfast; a mom swearing like a truck driver in the background, not knowing her son was not on mute; and a dad walking by his daughter's room in his underwear—ok, that was quite the sight.

I think one of my favorite's was when a student jumped on Google Classroom *late* as I was teaching the other students— already in progress. He jumps on, and says "Hi Mrs. M. I am on my way to the doctor with my mom." He is literally in the car, radio going on in the background, and mom is taking him to the doctor!

OK, these kids really learned A LOT during COVID-19 and remote learning.

The Big Kids would put themselves on *mute* with an image uploaded as their profile picture. So picture yourself, teaching to the class on the computer and looking at all these freakish images instead of *live human beings*. That was just fantastic!!! (UGH!)

Trying to teach a class *live* in the classroom with some students who came to school when it was allowed during COVID-19. Then having to go online with a computer in front of me and log on to Google Classroom with the rest of the class. So I am now teaching students *live* and students on the computer, remotely, from their homes.

Well, when I am trying to fix the Google Classroom glitches, I have several kindergartners running around in my classroom, thinking it's playtime because I haven't begun teaching yet. Yes, it was that crazy.

There was even a time a parent from home wrote a sign to me, "CANNOT HEAR YOU!!!!" My volume wasn't working on Google Classroom.

Stop the madness—everyone get back to school, in person!!!! (NOW!)

Please Lord, don't ever make me do that again—please, please, please.

My Titos expense went waaayyyyyy up during COVID-19 teaching.

I leave you now with some famous quotes from students across the land.

First grade morning meeting question of the day: "If you could only have one food, and one drink for the rest of your life, what would it be?"

"Lettuce and milk."
"Pizza and Fanta."

"Cookies and milk."

"A root beer float with an umbrella in the glass and a cheeseburger." (Ohhhh, now there's a high maintenance first grader. HA!)

"A blue slushy and pizza."

"An orange slushy and cookies."

Ok class, give me a word with a long O sound.
The best answer yet:
"Smoooooooooooooooooke pot."

"Mrs. M., I was on the toilet all day yesterday. I was pooping and puking. If you see me run out of the room today, don't worry. I just have to go to the bathroom real bad."

"OK!!!"

"My mommy was very happy with me yesterday...when I rubbed her feet, she gave me money."

"Mrs. Patti, I gotta peeeeeeeee—it's an emergenceeeeeeee."

"Mrs. Patti, how old are you...maybe 90...no, no, no wait...100?"

I usually wear my hair up when I teach; it's just easier. One day I had my hair down with a little makeup too, I believe. Well, this adorable preschool student comes up to me and says, "Mrs. Patti, you are like candy." (HA!)

A kindergartner out sick for a few days comes into my class with the following accomplishment:

"Mrs. Patti, I puked nine times yesterday!"

"I love the color poo-poo."

Me: "Pooh pooh?"

"No, poo-poo."

Me: "Pooh pooh?"
"Mrs. Patti, look at this crayon—this color..."
Me: "Ohhhhhh, purple!"

"My grandma is good friends with the pope, she lives near him too."

Me: "Oh really, where does your grandmother live?"

"Missouri." (HA!)

One last kindergartner joke:

Why did the chef go to jail?

Because he was beating the eggs. (HA!)

I truly hope you enjoyed the book. It's all light, in good fun, and most of all, giving you something to smile and laugh about in this crazy world.

Believe it or not, I love being a *sub*! Even with the daily, crazy stories. Most of these kids are amazing—most, not all, but most. (HA!)

Funny stories are good for the soul.

I hope your days are filled with memories of fun-filled stories that warm the heart.

Theeeeeeeeeeeeeeeeeeee End

Milton Keynes UK
Ingram Content Group UK Ltd.
UKRC031054220424
441552UK00002B/10

* 9 7 9 8 8 2 2 9 4 3 2 8 5 *